Christiana And Her Children

CHRISTIANA & HER CHILDREN

Go now, my little book, to every place
Where my first Pilgrim has but shown his face:
Call at their door. If any say, Who's there?
Then answer thou, Christiana is here.

John Bunyan

CHRISTIANA & HER CHILDREN

A MYSTERY PLAY

Adapted by Mrs Duncan Pearce

from

BUNYAN'S PILGRIM'S PROGRESS

TAITH Y PERERIN

Given for the first time in Wales, at the Town Hall,
Holyhead, 24 March 1914

LONGMANS GREEN AND COMPANY
39 PATERNOSTER ROW · LONDON
NEW YORK · BOMBAY · CALCUTTA AND MADRAS
1914

LETCHWORTH: PRINTED AT THE ARDEN PRESS

TO
HIS SERENE HIGHNESS THE RIGHT HONOURABLE
ADMIRAL PRINCE LOUIS OF BATTENBERG
G.C.B., G.C.V.O.
THIS MEMORIAL OF A WORK
UNDERTAKEN FOR THE BENEFIT OF
THE STANLEY HOME FOR SAILORS AT HOLYHEAD
IS BY PERMISSION DEDICATED

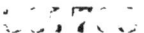

FOR ALL WE HAVE AND ARE

FOR all we have and are,
  For all our children's fate,
Stand up and meet the war.
The Hun is at the gate!
Our world has passed away
In wantonness o'erthrown.
There is nothing left to-day
But steel and fire and stone!
  Though all we knew depart,
  The old commandments stand:
  "In courage keep your heart,
  In strength lift up your hand."

Once more we hear the word
That sickened earth of old:
"No law except the Sword
Unsheathed and uncontrolled."
Once more it knits mankind,
Once more the nations go
To meet and break and bind
A crazed and driven foe.

Comfort, content, delight,
The ages' slow-bought gain,
They shrivelled in a night,
Only ourselves remain
To face the naked days
In silent fortitude,
Through perils and dismays
Renewed and re-renewed.
   Though all we made depart,
   The old commandments stand:
   "In patience keep your heart,
   In strength lift up your hand."

No easy hopes or lies
Shall bring us to our goal,
But iron sacrifice
Of body, will, and soul.
There is but one task for all—
For each one life to give.
Who stands if freedom fall?
Who dies if England live?

                      RUDYARD KIPLING.

[By permission of the Author.]

*" My Pilgrim's Book has travell'd sea and land,
Yet could I never come to understand
That it was slighted, or turn'd out of door
By any kingdom, were they rich or poor.
   In France and Flanders, where men kill each other,
My Pilgrim is esteem'd a friend, a brother."*

John Bunyan, 1684.

PREFACE

THAT the prose poem, which is so much nobler than most poetical poems after the Elizabethan age, should be used to help our sailors is more suitable than it seems. Bunyan was a Midland man, if ever there was one; and there is not, I think, in his wonderful fairy tale so much as a whisper of the sea. Yet he was of the sort that might have been a sailor as he was a soldier; and there is in his book a sort of knarled goodness such as sailors know. Or again, it might be counted an irony that the Puritan's tale should be turned into a stage play, and even a Miracle play; and adorned, as it is here, with all the medieval delight of the eye and dignity of the body, of which the Puritans despoiled themselves. Yet again, Bunyan was a dramatist if ever there was one: he could not have been long kept from what is called going on the stage. None were more full of Puritan purpose than the Scotch: but I number almost among my nursery traditions that a great Scotch mystic, the late George Macdonald, appeared as Great-heart. It is something of a tribute to him, both physically and spiritually, that it seemed natural to me even when I was a boy.

For Bunyan the Midlander was right. When we send forth our sailors, we do not fear the wide seas, but only the narrow river. Mere distances are not appalling; rather they are pleasing; productive of welcomes and of travellers' tales. The tenderness felt for sailors, by all that humanity that can be called human, is due to their daily proximity to that dark rivulet which Bunyan found flowing through Bedfordshire, and which flows through every land and sea. We love these men because they are always threatened; and we like any institution which may enable such threatened men to live long.

G. K. CHESTERTON.

CONTENTS

An Ideal Sailors' Home — *Frontispiece*
Dedication to H.S.H. Prince Louis of Battenberg — page 5
For All We Have And Are by Rudyard Kipling — 6
Preface by G. K. Chesterton — 9
Note on the Sailors' Home by Lord Kilbracken — 15
The Committee of the Mystery Play — 18
Players and their Parts — 19
Singers and Musicians — 20
The Music — 21
Introduction by Lady Verney — 23
Old Welsh Hymn — 27
Illustrations:
  Vision of Christian without his Burden — facing page 30
  Christiana welcomes the Heavenly Messenger — 32
  " Peace be to this House and Thee " — 34
  Christiana's Appeal — 36
  " I have good news " — 38
  Christiana awakes from her Dream — 40
  Christiana's Neighbours — 42
  By this time Christiana had got on her way — 44
  The Pilgrims at the Wicket Gate — 46
  Mercy outside the Wicket Gate — 48
  An Angel blesses Mercy — 50
  Weary Pilgrims lie down to sleep in the House Beautiful — 52
  Vision of an Angel appears to the Pilgrims — 54
  In the House Beautiful Mercy sits at work — 56
  Greatheart as Guide — 58
  Vanity Fair — 60
  The Watcher — 62

Illustrations—continued
The Passing of Christiana	64
The Messenger	66
Vision of Reunion	68
The Angel's Welcome at the Beautiful Gate of the City	70
Envoi by Lady Ritchie, daughter of William Makepeace Thackeray	73
"1914" by Mrs Emery Walker	74

An Ideal Sailors Home

The Stanley Sailors Home at Holyhead (affiliated to the Missions to Seamen) which has benefitted by the production of this Play was erected when H.R.H. The Prince of Wales (King Edward VII) visited Holyhead to declare the Breakwater open in 1873

During the past year over 3000 men and boys made use of this Sailors Home which for more than 40 years has done admirable work among the seafaring population of Holyhead

Emery Walker (a witness from a passing ship of the opening in 1873)

Chairman of Committee
Rear Admiral J. Leslie Burr C.M.G. M.V.O.
Captain of the Port, Holyhead

Hon Secretary and Treasurer
Rice R. Williams, Esq., Stanley House, Holyhead

A NOTE ON THE SAILORS' HOME

NO Englishman needs to be reminded of the debt which we owe to the Royal Navy: least of all in such times as those in which we are now living (October, 1914). But the debt which we owe to the sailors of our Mercantile Marine, though not so obvious and palpable, is scarcely less; the services which they render us are so continuous, so essential, and, at the same time, to landsmen, so inconspicuous, that we almost take them for granted like the air we breathe; and it is only now and then that we are reminded, perhaps by a paragraph in a newspaper, that without those services we could not exist either as a nation or as individuals, and that their cessation, even for a few months, would mean ruin, starvation and misery for rich and poor alike throughout the United Kingdom. And it must be remembered that even when active service is over these men can and do play a useful part in the work which never ceases in our harbours and along our coasts. It is they who man our lifeboats, and in many other ways minister to the needs of those who are still in the "fighting line" of that peaceful warfare which Englishmen are for ever carrying on in all parts of the world to which the sea can float them.

These services deserve our recognition: and no form of recognition is more beneficial or more acceptable than that of Sailors' Homes, where young and old can meet in comfort and enjoy a well-earned rest away from the too-well-known temptations of seaport towns. It is not easy to over-estimate the value of a clean, refined, well-managed place of resort where all the social influences are good and where shipwrecked crews find a hospitable shelter, good food, dry clothing, and every care and attention that they can require until they can be dispatched to their various destinations.

On the rocky shore of Holyhead Harbour, close to the Lifeboat Station and within easy reach of the sea, a home of this kind, "THE STANLEY SAILORS' HOME," has done its patriotic work for more than forty years, and has been a haven of rest and happiness to many a sailor, who has gone away from it clothed and refreshed, strengthened in mind and body and ready to risk his life once more in the pursuit of his calling and in the service of mankind. Charles Dickens has described the wreck of the "Royal Charter," driven on to the shores of Anglesey and shattered by the great storm of 1859; and when we think of the work done by this Home for Sailors, and of the ministrations of the chaplains who have been attached to it, it is impossible not to be reminded of the words in which he speaks of the devoted Welsh rector, the Revd Stephen Roose Hughes, who then did such noble work for those who suffered: "Convocations, conferences, and the like will do a great deal for religion I dare say (and heaven send they may), but I doubt if they will ever do their Master's service half so well . . . as the heavens have seen it done in this bleak spot upon the rugged coast of Wales."

It was for the benefit of this work that the undertaking described in the following pages was attempted.

KILBRACKEN.

> "*Sailor, what of the debt we owe you?*
> *Day or night is the peril more?*
> *Who so dull that he fails to know you,*
> *Sleepless guard of our island shore?*"
>
> A.S.
(From *The Times*, by permission of the Author.)

THE MYSTERY PLAY
OF
CHRISTIANA & HER CHILDREN

COMMITTEE

Chairman: Mr Williams, Boston House
Hon. Secretary: Mrs Rice Williams

Lady Goodrich	Mrs Oswald Hobbs
Miss Adeane	Miss Owen Jones
Miss Burr	Miss MacKinstry
Miss Elliott	Mrs Gwilym Owen
Mrs Fox-Pitt	Mrs Fox Russell
Miss Hughes	Miss Taylor

Mrs Turner

Admiral Burr, C.M.G.	Mr David Jones
Mr O. B. Edwards	Mr Learmouth
Mr Oswald Hobbs	Rev. F. Watkin-Davies

PRODUCER OF PLAY
Mr Cecil Kinnaird

DESIGNER OF COSTUMES
Mr Herbert North, Llanfairfechan, N. Wales

PROLOGUE

Spoken in the Afternoon by Professor J. E. Lloyd,
     of the University College of North Wales
and in the Evening by Mr W. H. Williams

PLAYERS & THEIR PARTS

Christian	Mr Spencer
Christiana	Miss Mary Heaton
Mercy	Miss Burrows
Matthew ⎫ Sons of	Glyn Williams
Samuel ⎬ Christiana	M. Tywyn Jones
James ⎭	A. Ball
Greatheart	Mr O. Hobbs
Interpreter	Mr Learmouth
Heavenly Messenger	Mr Owen
Mrs Timorous	Miss Eva Burr
Mrs Knownothing	Miss Hugh Jones
Mrs Inconsiderate	Miss Owen Jones
Prudence	Mrs Oswald Hobbs
Innocence	Miss Fox Pitt
Piety	Mrs Evan Jones
Angel	Mrs Erskine Loch
Shining Ones	Mrs Trevor & Mrs Evan Jones
Grand Ladies	{ Mrs Arch Jones, Miss Taylor, Miss Talbot & Miss Scheizer
Dancing Girls	{ Miss Noel Dolling, Miss Plews, Miss Dawson, Miss Bridle, Miss Sydney Lloyd & Miss Henry
Dancers and Gamblers	{ Mr Edwards, Mr Learmouth, Mr W. H. Owen & Mr Sorge
Flower Girl	Miss Telfer
Beggar Boy	Wilfred Nash
Miser	Mr Williams
Man with Rake	Mr Bailey

Groups photographed by Mr Wickens, Bangor
Single figures by Miss Dorothy Hickling, London

SINGERS & MUSICIANS

Conductor: Mr T. Price
(Late Director of Music in Repton School)

SINGERS

Soloists	Mrs Gwynneddon Davies, Miss Singleton, Mr David Jones & Mr Owen
Sopranos	Lady Goodrich, Miss Bellis, Miss Evans, Miss F. Davies, Miss Irene Davies, Miss Gregson, Miss E. Hughes, Miss Humphreys, Miss Singleton, Miss Peters, Miss Grace Jones, Miss Roberts, Miss Williams & Miss C. Williams
Contraltos	Mrs Griffiths, Mrs Williams, Miss M. L. Williams, Miss Owen & Miss N. Jones
Tenors	Mr R. W. Edwards, Mr Griffiths, Mr Owen, Mr Learmouth, Mr Roberts & Mr Rowlands
Basses	Mr J. Edwards, Mr Osmond, Mr W. H. Jones, Mr David Jones & Mr Ellis Roberts

MUSICIANS

Violins	Miss Agnes Jones (Leader), Miss Polly Jones, Mrs Doughty
Viola	Miss Gwendolen Pryce
Violoncellos	Miss Evelyn Pryce, Mrs Hale, Miss Margaret Rae
Double Bass	Mrs O. Hobbs
Piano	Miss Adah Williams
Harmonium	Miss Owen Jones

THE MUSIC

THE incidental music was taken principally from Dr A. R. Gaul's "Holy City" (this composer died shortly before the rehearsals at Holyhead began), and the orchestral parts were kindly lent by his daughter, Miss Lilian Gaul. Choruses and solos from this cantata accompanied the Pilgrims throughout, except between Scenes 2 and 3, when Massenet's "Prelude" suggested Mercy's first vague yearnings, and the hymn, "Come unto Me, ye weary," fitly illustrated Scene 5, where the tired Pilgrims slowly travelled on the road.

Later in the Play, Handel's solo, "Angels ever bright and fair," was sung as the Angels appeared above the sleeping Pilgrims in "the House Beautiful."

During the passing of the Pilgrims through the "Valley of the Shadows," its unknown terrors were expressed by the strange discords and unexpected progressions of the "Valse Triste," by Sibelius; while in the procession and scene representing "Vanity Fair," dance music and an old English folk-song were introduced.

A most effective contrast was gained by the return to the harmonious concords of the "Holy City," and its last number, "List to the Cherubic Host," gave a triumphant note and formed a poetic ending to the final Vision.

INTRODUCTION

A HUNDRED years ago, and much earlier, the *Pilgrim's Progress*, in its Welsh dress, held an honoured place beside the family Bible, in the chimney-corner of the farm and the cottage in Wales. In the little grey stone manor-houses of Anglesey, the Bible, Bunyan, and Virgil were the fireside companions of the old squire and magistrate; but the flood of cheap literature, in which so many treasures have been submerged, seems to have swept "Taith y Pererin" out of the people's homes. A quest made in the neighbourhood of Holyhead last Christmas scarcely revealed a copy; it was a traditional name known to "Nain," our grandmother, but without meaning for the young people and the children of the present age.

To revive interest in the *Pilgrim's Progress*, and to present to her neighbours a series of lovely scenes full of devotional meaning, had been a cherished dream of Miss Adeane's for several years past.

The enterprise was an arduous one, and depended for its success on the patient and enthusiastic co-operation of a number of workers, willing to be trained in many rehearsals, till the singing, the elocution, and the dramatization of this beautiful Mystery Play could be presented as a perfect whole. But all this was happily accomplished. During the performance, the vivacity and freshness with which the story moved along; the richness of the colour-scheme; the apparent spontaneity of the dialogue; and the refinement and finish of the acting produced so marvellous an effect—that the crowded audience watched in a tense silence, scarcely conscious of its details, the vision that was being unrolled before their eyes.

The absence of any theatrical adjuncts contributed greatly to the feeling of reality which possessed us. The actors were so close by, they came at times down the wide flight of steps into our very midst, and wheeled to right and left and vanished again. Or they would suddenly appear in procession, starting from the back of the hall and pass through us, intent only on the business of their pilgrimage. When the dim religious light burnt very low, sweet strains of music, and voices harmoniously blended, reached us from unseen performers; and when the light gleamed brilliantly again on a vision of Shining Ones, with white, glistening wings—the silence in which they moved, as they brought dreams to troubled sleepers, and blessings to weary children, was more impressive than any words.

Most lovers of the Pilgrim story would perchance have turned to the first book for the more dramatic episodes; the " Progress " of Christian is so strenuous and of such varied and sustained interest—but in the Women's sequel to the tale, there is a gentleness, a sense of pity for the weaker and more timid wayfarers, and a playful sympathy with children—"When little tripping maidens follow God"—which lends itself perhaps better to leisurely and artistic presentation than the earlier and sterner narrative.

"The young person whose name was Dull" was never allowed to occupy the stage for a moment, and there was much of homely humour in feminine preparations for the journey, amid the interruptions of carping visitors; and much tossing about of fine clothes, and snatching of crimson and gold draperies from one to another, when Christiana's lady-neighbours realized that she had been such "a fantastic fool" as to abandon her home and all the costly apparel over which they were wrangling.

Mrs Timorous, Mrs Knownothing and Mrs Inconsiderate, staggering out of the house with the spoils each so grudged to the other, formed an amusing picture, but how can one describe the sustained earnestness and inspired resolution of the lady who personated Christiana; or the pathos of "young Mercy's" figure, bowed down with the sense of her own unworthiness, without the assurance of a welcome that sustained her friend—yet so determined to bear her company, and to "take what shall follow."

Greatheart, in shining armour, was a splendid personage, with his protecting gentleness to the weak and weary; the little boys with their packs, their bright faces and artless prattle aroused enthusiasm at their every appearance—but the success of the whole depended on the arduous parts of the two women, Christiana and Mercy.

The most dramatic moment of the Mystery Play came with a sudden burst of loud laughter and music, and a rabble-rout of dancers and jesters breaking in upon the hushed discourse and quiet garb of the pilgrims—and while *they* were huddled up in a corner, the mad revels of Vanity Fair were carried on with the noisiest accompaniments. In the very front of the games and the dancing, sat a man at the top of the steps, a dark silhouette of Avarice, scattering his money and raking it together again with long skinny fingers. Little Matthew was attracted by the chink and glitter of the gold, till he saw a beggar-child roughly repulsed by the gambler, when he fled in terror to the shelter of his mother's skirts. In effect and sentiment the contrast was all that Bunyan himself could have desired to point his moral. The strong protest of the Puritan was much needed at the time—and is still needed—where plays and dancing are degraded by wrong associations which destroy the pure spirit of wholesome mirth.

But in this representation the girls in green draperies were so gay and graceful, and the men in Tudor coats and caps of black and crimson were so happy in their dancing, the flower garlands were so fragrant, and all the fun and frolic of the fair were so innocent and harmless, that the most anxious conscience could only rejoice in a scene of such artistic beauty and happy, guileless merriment.

The closing scenes raised us once more to the Enchanted Ground and the Holy City. Christiana lay a-dying, Mercy and the boys kneeling beside her bed, Greatheart on guard with bowed head—a sad parting seemed imminent—when in the spirit of

> "Say not good night, but in some brighter clime
> Bid me good morning"—

the room was filled with beckoning, Shining Ones; Christiana arose and followed them through the wicket-gate by which the visions came, and an angel shut it behind her.

Another pause, and one more silent tableau: Christiana knelt re-united to her husband, her hand in his—the grand old Welsh hymn, "O Fryniau Caersalem," was taken up by many voices, and then the great company went out into the gathering darkness with a sense that it had been good to be there.

MARGARET M. VERNEY.

OLD WELSH HYMN

O Fryniau Caersalem ceir gweled
  Holl daith yr anialwch i gyd;
Pryd hyny daw troion yr yrfa
Yn felus i lanw ein bryd;
Cawn edrych ar'stormydd ac ofnau,
Ac angeu dychrynllyd, a'r bedd,
A ninnau'n ddiangol o'u cyrhaedd
Yn nofio mewn cariad a hedd!

TRANSLATION.

FROM Salem's fair heights shall the ransom'd
  Look back on the wilderness past.
The sight of the toils and the dangers
Will sweeten our rest at the last.
The thought of fierce tempests and trials
The terrors of death and the grave,
But heighten our rapture of worship
Of Him who was mighty to save—
What joy when we reach the Blest City
To muse on the deserts we trod
For there dwell the weary and wayworn
At rest in the Bosom of God.

                A. WALTER THOMAS (Morfydd Eryri).

CHRISTIANA'S DREAM

THEN SHE THOUGHT SHE SAW CHRISTIAN, HER HUSBAND, IN A PLACE OF BLISS, AMONG MANY IMMORTALS.

VISION OF CHRISTIAN WITHOUT HIS BURDEN

CHRISTIANA: " IF THOU COMEST IN GOD'S NAME, COME IN.'

CHRISTIANA WELCOMES THE HEAVENLY MESSENGER

CHRISTIANA: "O WHO ART THOU WHO COMEST IN THE DAWN, WITH SHINING EYES AND GENTLE SPEECH?"

HEAVENLY MESSENGER: "PEACE BE TO THIS HOUSE AND THEE."

CHRISTIANA CRIED: " SIR, WILL YOU CARRY ME AND MY CHILDREN WITH YOU, THAT WE ALSO MAY GO AND WORSHIP THE KING? "

CHRISTIANA'S APPEAL TO THE HEAVENLY MESSENGER

" THE KING WHO LOVES US ALL SO WELL HAS SENT A LETTER TO ME, AS I WOKE FROM SLEEP—TO TELL ME TO PACK UP AND COME WITH YOU."

CHRISTIANA: "I HAVE GOOD NEWS."

CHRISTIANA: "I WAS DREAMING LAST NIGHT THAT I SAW HIM. O THAT MY SOUL WERE WITH HIM."

CHRISTIANA AWAKES FROM HER DREAM

MRS KNOWNOTHING, MRS INCONSIDERATE AND MRS TIMOROUS TURNING OVER CHRISTIANA'S POSSESSIONS: "HOLD THEE, GOOD FRIEND. SHE SAID WE WOULD DIVIDE, AND YOU SEEM MAKING ALL YOUR OWN."

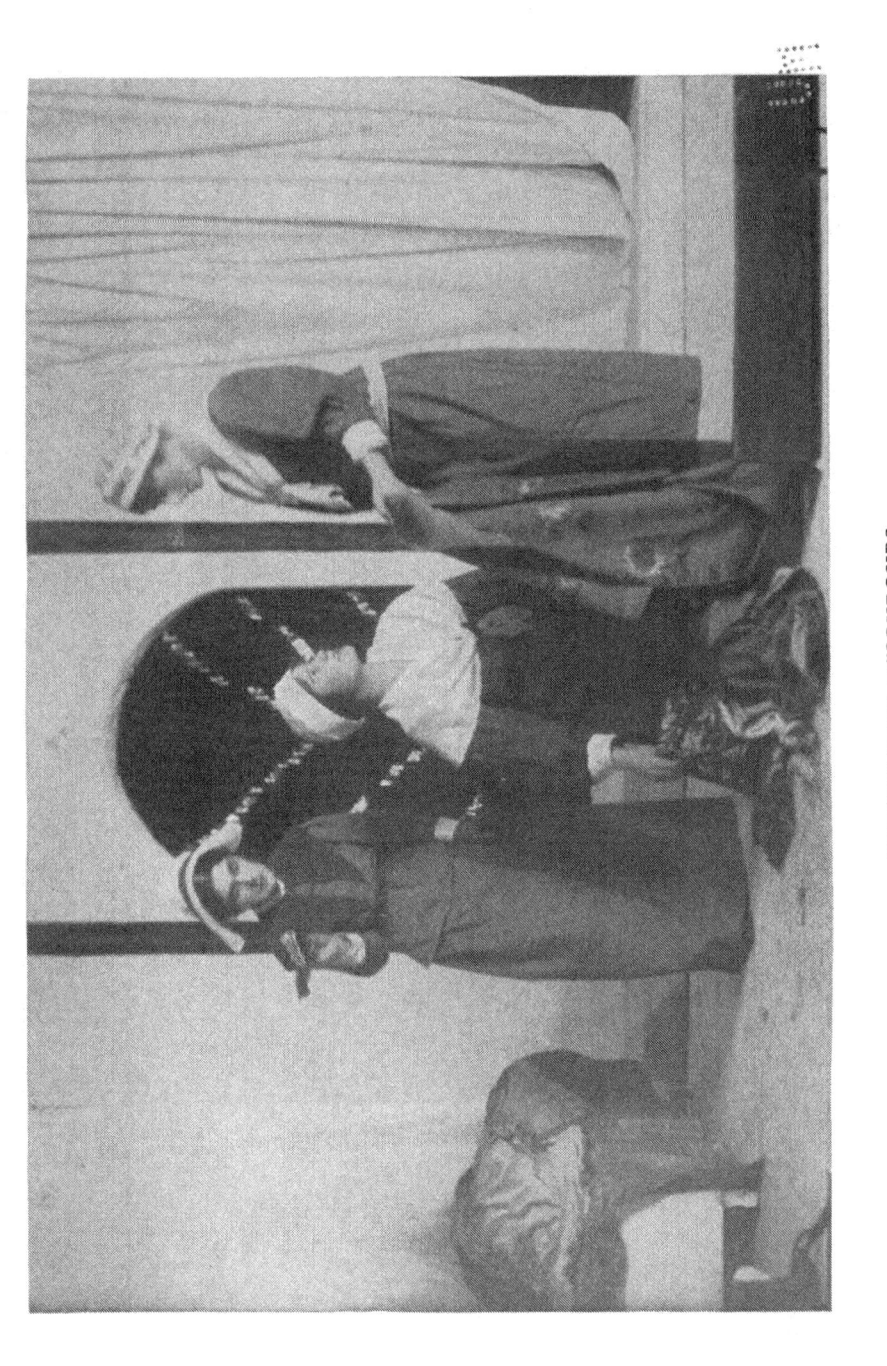

CHRISTIANA'S NEIGHBOURS

AT THE WICKET GATE CHRISTIANA BEGAN TO KNOCK. SHE KNOCKED AND KNOCKED AGAIN. THEN SAID THE KEEPER OF THE GATE:
" WHENCE COME YE, AND WHAT IS IT YOU WOULD HAVE? "
SHE ANSWERED: " I AM CHRISTIANA, ONCE THE WIFE OF CHRISTIAN, THAT NOW IS GOTTEN ABOVE."

"BY THIS TIME CHRISTIANA HAD GOT ON HER WAY."

WITH THAT THE KEEPER OF THE GATE DID MARVEL: "WHAT, IS SHE NOW BECOME A PILGRIM THAT BUT AWHILE AGO ABHORRED THAT LIFE?"

SHE BOWED HER HEAD AND SAID: "YEA, AND SO ARE THESE MY SWEET BABES ALSO."

THEN HE LET HER IN, AND SAID ALSO: "SUFFER THE LITTLE CHILDREN TO COME UNTO ME."

WITH THAT HE SHUT THE GATE.

THE PILGRIMS AT THE WICKET GATE

" AH ME! AH ME! I AM SHUT OUT ALONE.
   HE NEVER SAID I COULD COME IN WITH THEM."

MERCY OUTSIDE THE WICKET GATE

"PEACE BE TO THEE."

AN ANGEL BLESSES MERCY

MERCY DREAMS OF AN ANGEL'S VISIT AND WAKES UP LAUGHING.
SHE KNOWS NOW THAT SHE IS WELCOME TO THE HEAVENLY CITY.

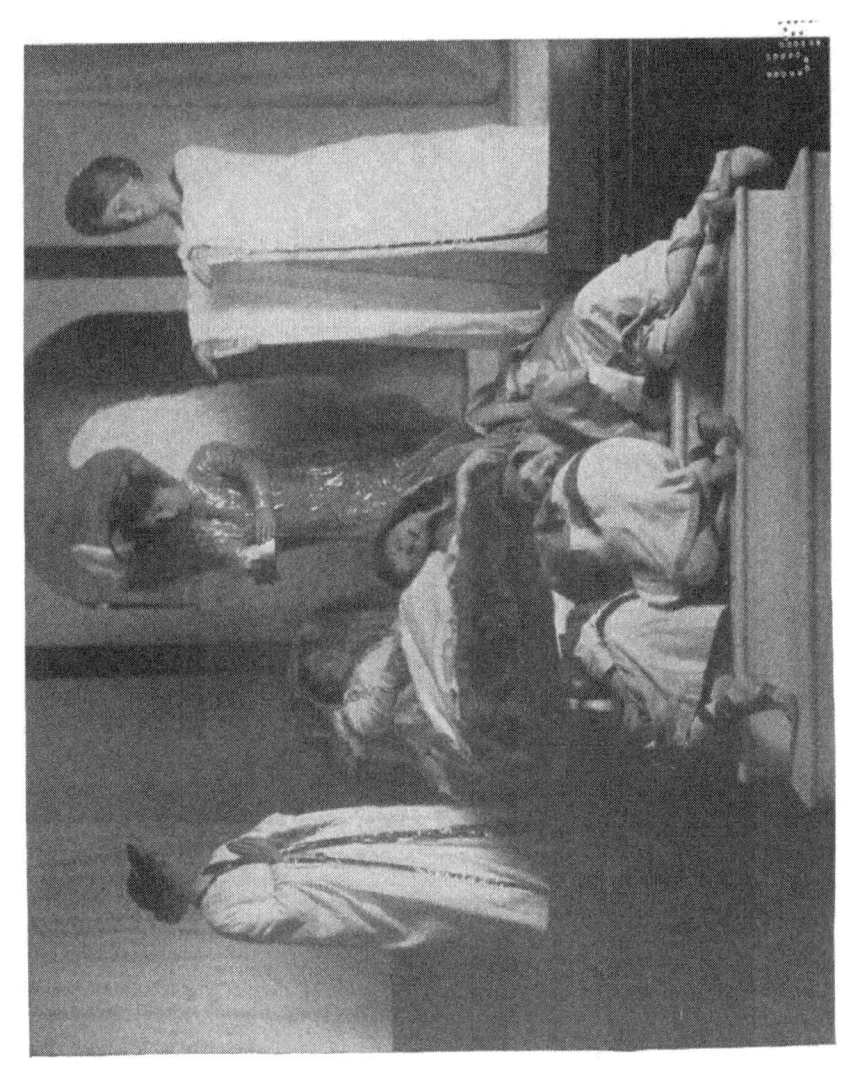

THE WEARY PILGRIMS LIE DOWN TO SLEEP IN THE HOUSE CALLED BEAUTIFUL

" METHOUGHT AN ANGEL CAME, STATELY AND TALL, WITH SWEET AND LOVING EYES, SHINING LIKE STARS."

VISION OF AN ANGEL APPEARS TO THE PILGRIMS

MERCY: "HARK, DO YOU HEAR A VOICE?"
CHRISTIANA: "YES, IT IS, I BELIEVE, A SOUND OF MUSIC FOR JOY THAT WE ARE HERE."
MERCY: "WONDERFUL! MUSIC IN THE HOUSE, MUSIC IN THE HEART AND MUSIC ALSO IN HEAVEN, FOR JOY THAT WE ARE HERE."

IN THE "HOUSE BEAUTIFUL" MERCY SITS AT WORK

THE INTERPRETER THEN CALLED FOR ONE, GREATHEART, AND BADE HIM TAKE SWORD, HELMET AND SHIELD. SO HE TOOK HIS WEAPONS AND WENT BEFORE THEM. THEN SAID THE YOUNGEST OF THE BOYS: " PRAY, SIR, BE PERSUADED TO GO WITH US, BECAUSE WE ARE SO WEAK AND THE WAY SO DANGEROUS AS IT IS."

GREATHEART AS GUIDE: "NOW WE ARE SAFE, AND HE OUR FRIEND IS HERE."

"A GOODLY TOWN WHERE MANY PEOPLE DWELL, BUT FEW WITH FACES SET TOWARDS THAT LAND TO WHICH WE ARE BOUND."

VANITY FAIR

"THERE IS NOW A LEGION OF SHINING ONES JUST COME TO TOWN BY WHICH WE KNOW THAT THERE ARE MANY MORE PILGRIMS UPON THE ROAD, FOR HERE THEY COME TO WAIT FOR THEM, AND COMFORT THEM AFTER THEIR SORROW."

THE WATCHER: "MANY PILGRIMS WENT OVER THE WATER AND WERE LET IN AT THE GOLDEN GATES TO-DAY."

" NOW THE DAY DREW ON THAT CHRISTIANA MUST BE GONE . . . . WHILE SHE LAY THERE AND WAITED FOR THE GOOD HOUR, MESSENGERS CAME FROM THE CELESTIAL CITY FOR THE WIFE OF CHRISTIAN THE PILGRIM."

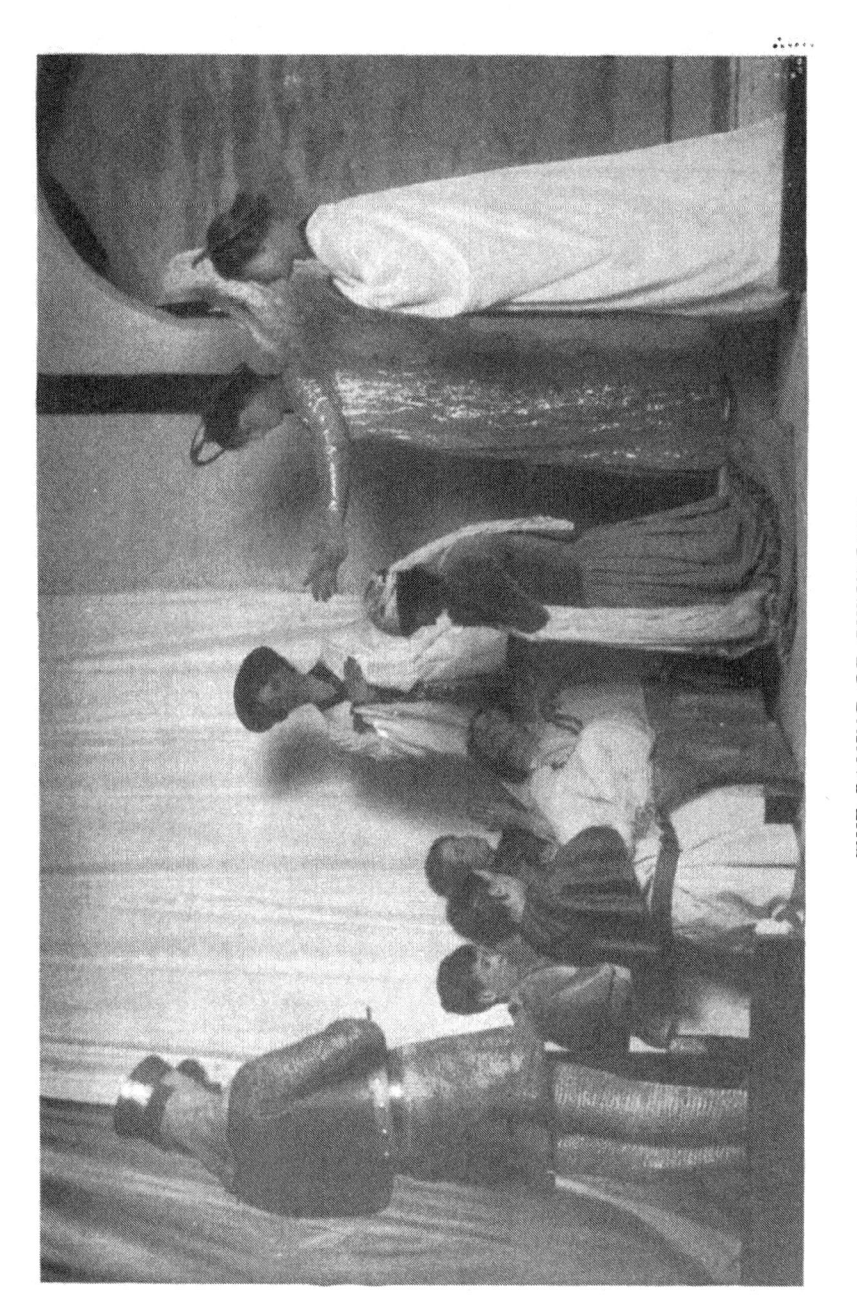

THE PASSING OF CHRISTIANA

"I BRING THEE GOOD TIDINGS: THE MASTER CALLETH FOR THEE."

THE MESSENGER

" THERE IS CHRISTIAN THY HUSBAND . . . . EVER BEHOLDING THAT FACE THAT DOTH MINISTER LIFE TO BEHOLDERS; AND THEY WILL ALL BE GLAD WHEN THEY SHALL HEAR THE SOUND OF THY FEET STEP OVER THY FATHER'S THRESHOLD."

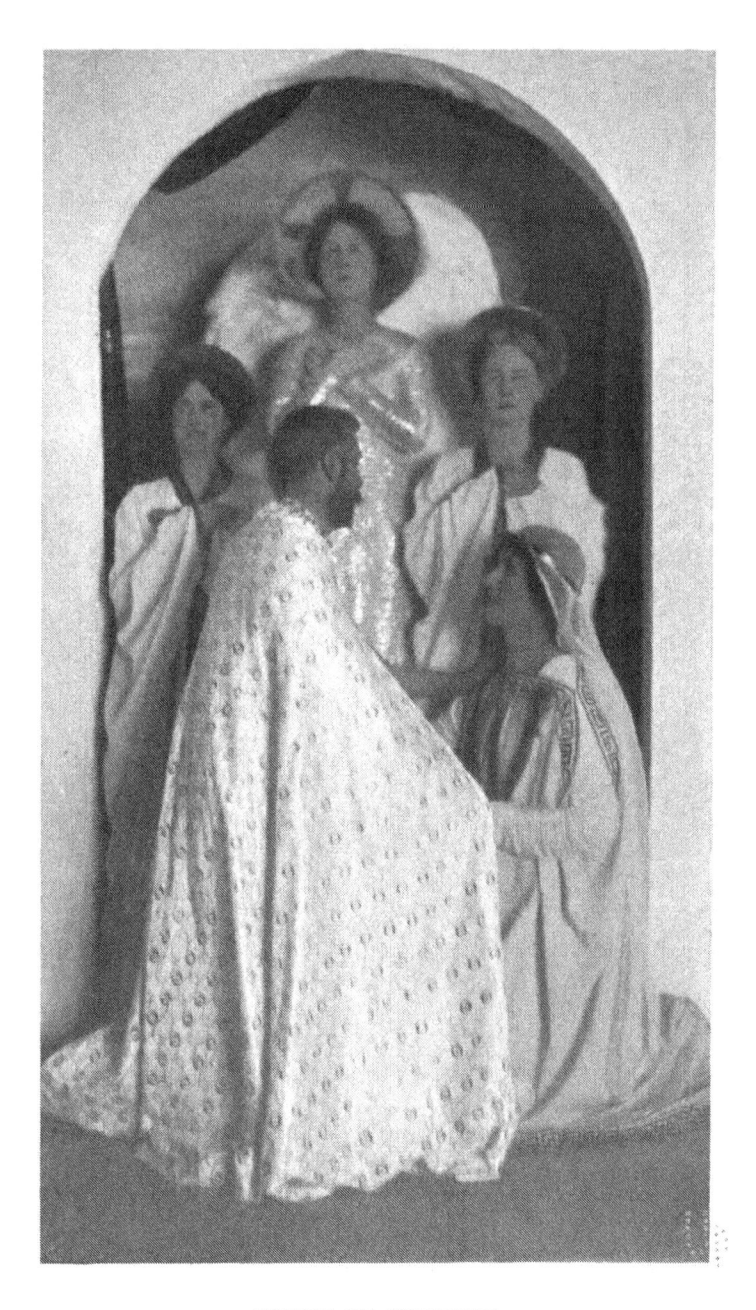

VISION OF REUNION

THE PILGRIMS' QUESTION: "WHAT MUST WE DO IN THIS HOLY PLACE?"
TO WHOM IT WAS ANSWERED: "YOU MUST THEN RECEIVE THE COMFORTS OF ALL YOUR TOIL, AND HAVE JOY FOR ALL YOUR SORROW; YOU MUST REAP WHAT YOU HAVE SOWN, EVEN THE FRUIT OF ALL YOUR PRAYERS AND TEARS AND SUFFERINGS FOR THE KING BY THE WAY: FOR THERE YOU SHALL SEE HIM AS HE IS."

THE ANGEL'S WELCOME AT THE BEAUTIFUL GATE OF THE CITY

ENVOI

THERE are times when some of us may realize that we are old and that the silver cord is loosed, and that river coming nearer and nearer from which Christiana beckoned farewell with so much courage and dignity; not less beautiful and stately I think is the leave-taking of Mr Ready-to-Halt, who sent for Mr Valiant to make his will, and because he had nothing else, bequeathed his crutches and his hundred warm wishes to those who should survive him, and his last words were, "Welcome life," as he went his way.

ANNIE RITCHIE.

1914

BECAUSE *our hearts are torn with grief*
  For friends and kindred slain,
More eager we to bring relief,
  Lest some may call in vain

For aid against the treacherous Sea,
  Who gathers to her breast,
With all-alluring witchery,
  Our bravest and our best.

She takes of human life her toll;
  None may dispute her claim;
And each inscribed upon the roll
  Must answer to his name.

His standard-bearers let us be
  Who died to save the lost,
And from the clutches of the Sea
  Rescue the tempest-tossed.

MARY GRACE WALKER.